FAMOUS SHIPWRECKS

SOUTHERN OCEAN SHIPWRECKS

by Michelle Parkin

pogo

Ideas for Parents and Teachers

Pogo Books let children practice reading informational text while introducing them to nonfiction features such as headings, labels, sidebars, maps, and diagrams, as well as a table of contents, glossary, and index.

Carefully leveled text with a strong photo match offers early fluent readers the support they need to succeed.

Before Reading

- "Walk" through the book and point out the various nonfiction features. Ask the student what purpose each feature serves.
- Look at the glossary together. Read and discuss the words.

Read the Book

- Have the child read the book independently.
- Invite him or her to list questions that arise from reading.

After Reading

- Discuss the child's questions. Talk about how he or she might find answers to those questions.
- Prompt the child to think more. Ask: What are some dangers of sailing in the Southern Ocean? What can ships do to stay safe?

Pogo Books are published by Jump!
5357 Penn Avenue South
Minneapolis, MN 55419
www.jumplibrary.com

Library of Congress Cataloging-in-Publication Data is available at www.loc.gov or upon request from the publisher.

ISBN: 979-8-88996-671-5 (hardcover)
ISBN: 979-8-88996-672-2 (paperback)
ISBN: 979-8-88996-673-9 (ebook)

Editor: Alyssa Sorenson
Designer: Anna Peterson

Photo Credits: Falklands Maritime Heritage Trust/ZUMA Press, Inc./Alamy, cover, 14–15; Danita Delimont/Alamy, 1; Willem Tims/Shutterstock, 3; titoOnz/Shutterstock, 4; Cultura Creative Ltd/Alamy, 5; aczerska/iStock, 6; Gerald Corsi/iStock, 7; De Agostini/Getty, 8–9; Posnov/Getty, 10–11; IanDagnall Computing/Alamy, 12–13; Michael Nolan/Age Fotostock, 16–17; Harvepino/Shutterstock, 18 (Earth); Yurij Omelchenko/Shutterstock, 18 (satellite); polarman/Shutterstock, 19; Tetyana Dotsenko/Shutterstock, 20–21; VichoT/iStock, 23.

Printed in the United States of America at Corporate Graphics in North Mankato, Minnesota.

TABLE OF CONTENTS

CHAPTER 1

WELCOME TO THE SOUTHERN OCEAN

The Southern Ocean circles Antarctica. It is also called the Antarctic Ocean.

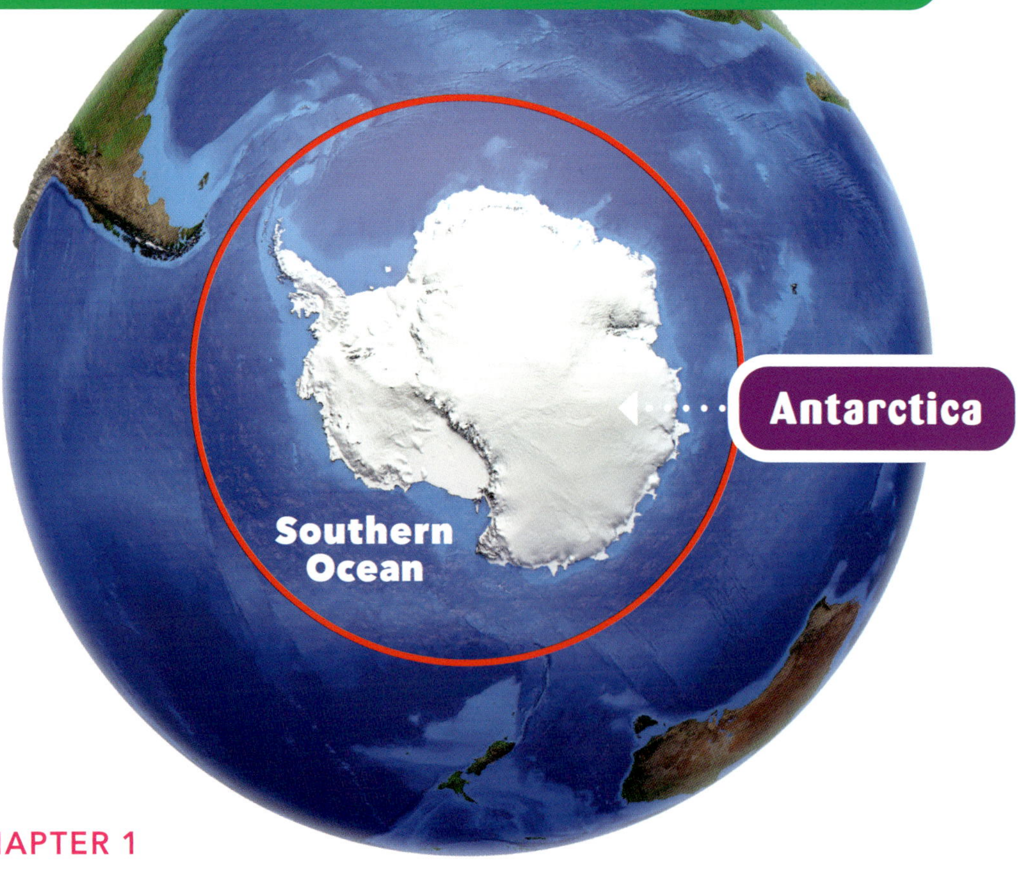

This ocean is very cold. **Icebergs** float in it all year.

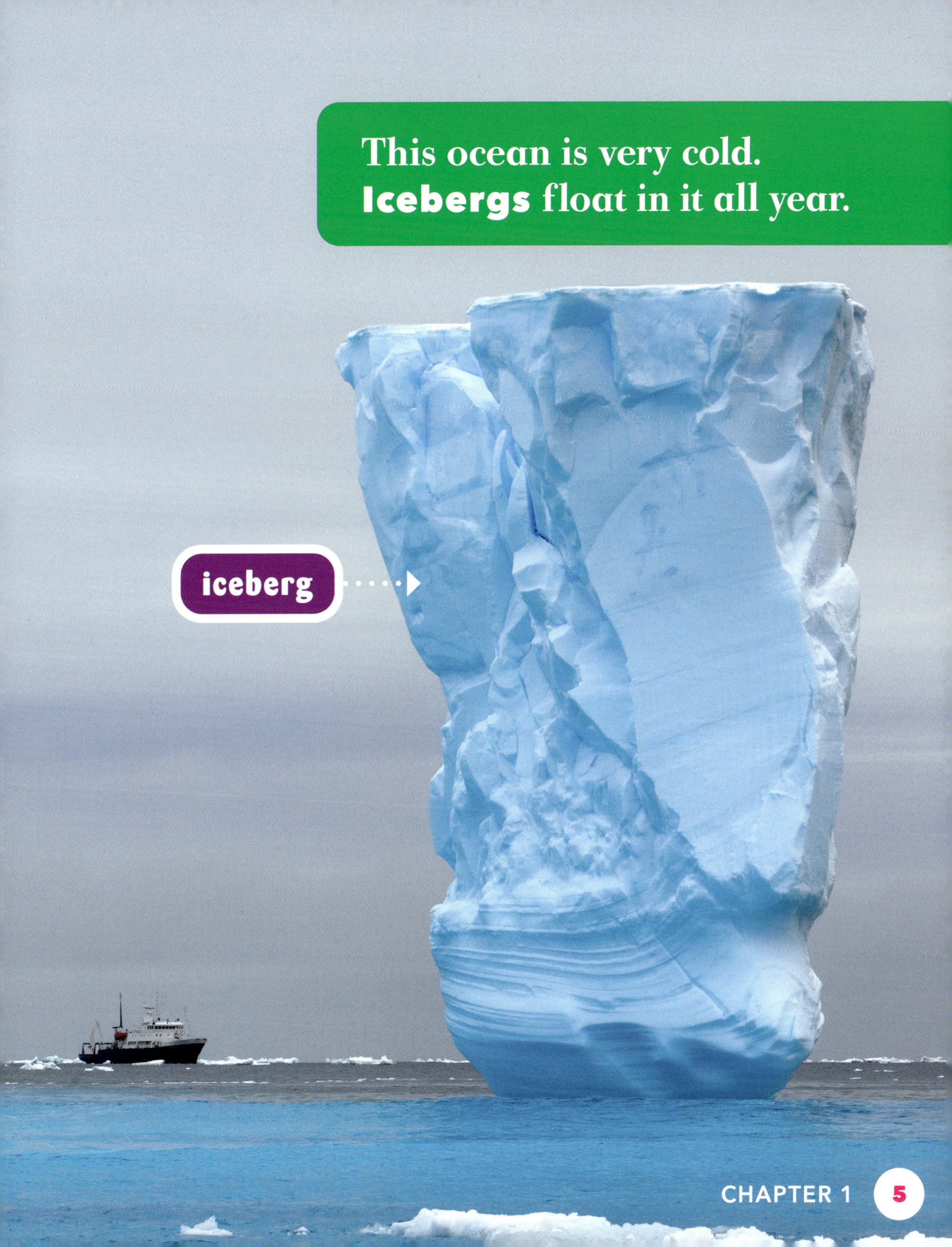

CHAPTER 2

ICY WATERS

Ships crash into the Southern Ocean's ice. They get stuck in it. The ocean's **currents** and strong winds **damage** ships.

The Drake Passage is between South America and Antarctica. It is one of the most dangerous places for ships. Why? Waves can be 40 feet (12 meters) high!

In 1819, the ship *San Telmo* was in the Drake Passage. A strong storm broke the ship apart. It sank. Pieces of a **shipwreck** were found a few months later. They may have been from the missing *San Telmo*.

DID YOU KNOW?

San Telmo's **crew** may have been the first people to die in Antarctica.

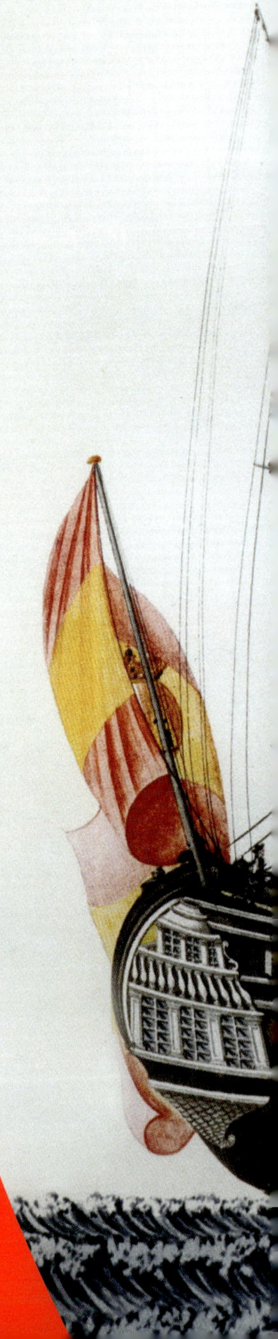

San Telmo

Governoren

Governoren was a large **whaling ship**. In January 1915, it sailed near Antarctica. Someone on board knocked over a lamp. It started a fire. Soon, the whole ship was in flames. Another ship **rescued** the crew. But *Governoren* couldn't be saved. Today, people visit the wreck. Part of it sticks out of the water.

WHAT DO YOU THINK?

People dive down to see the part of *Governoren* that is underwater. They need a lot of experience diving in cold water. Why do you think that is?

Ernest Shackleton was an **explorer**. He wanted to cross Antarctica. In December 1914, HMS *Endurance* set sail. But the ship got trapped in ice. Shackleton and the crew stayed on the ship for almost one year. They hoped the ship would break free. But in October 1915, ice pushed harder against the wooden ship. *Endurance* cracked. The crew left the ship. They set up camp on the ice. The ship filled with water. On November 21, 1915, it sank.

DID YOU KNOW?

There were 28 people on *Endurance*. All were rescued by August 1916.

HMS
Endurance

TAKE A LOOK!

Endurance is the Southern Ocean's most famous shipwreck. Take a look at the timeline of its journey!

DECEMBER 5, 1914
Endurance leaves the island of South Georgia and heads for Antarctica.

JANUARY 18, 1915
Endurance gets trapped in ice.

OCTOBER 27, 1915
The crew leaves the ship. They make camp on the ice.

NOVEMBER 21, 1915
Endurance sinks.

DECEMBER 29, 1915
The crew makes a new camp on floating ice. The ice moves them north.

APRIL 9, 1916
The crew lands on Elephant Island in three **lifeboats**.

APRIL 24, 1916
Shackleton and some others leave the island to find help.

MAY 20, 1916
Shackleton finds help in South Georgia.

AUGUST 30, 1916
The rest of the crew is rescued from Elephant Island.

MARCH 2022
Endurance is found.

The *Endurance* shipwreck wasn't found until 2022. This was more than 100 years after it sank! People used **sonar** and underwater vehicles to find it. The ship was in good shape. Why? Not many creatures in the Southern Ocean eat wood.

MS *Explorer* was a **cruise ship**. In November 2007, 154 people were on the ship. It hit ice hidden underwater. It ripped a hole in the ship. The ship took on water. It tipped to the side. People escaped in lifeboats. Another ship helped them. It took 20 hours for *Explorer* to sink.

MS *Explorer*

CHAPTER 3

SAILING THE SOUTHERN OCEAN TODAY

Satellites in space take images of the Southern Ocean. The images show where sea ice is. Ships move around the ice. Crew members use radios. They call people on land if they need help.

Some ships are made to sail through icy waters. **Icebreakers** cut through ice. They bring scientists to the Southern Ocean so they can study it.

More people are sailing on the Southern Ocean. They want to see Antarctica. They try to stay safe. But accidents happen. Will the Southern Ocean have more shipwrecks in the future?

WHAT DO YOU THINK?

Some people want to see Antarctica. The trip can be dangerous. Would you risk sailing on the icy ocean?

QUICK FACTS & TOOLS

WHERE THEY SANK IN THE SOUTHERN OCEAN

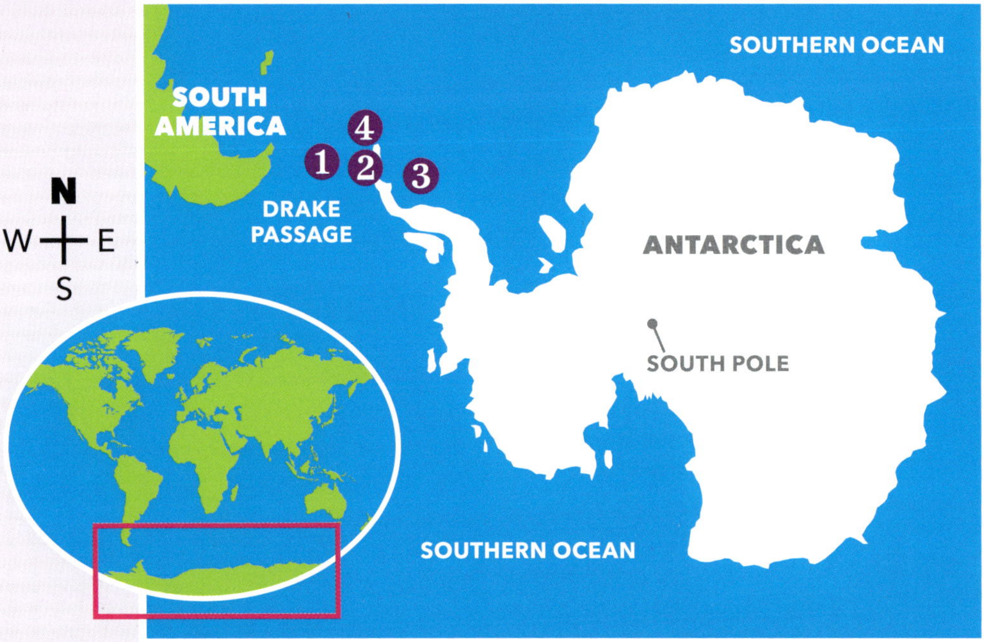

1. *San Telmo* sank in the Drake Passage in 1819. The exact location of the sinking is unknown.
2. *Governoren* caught fire and sank in 1915. People visit the shipwreck today.
3. HMS *Endurance* was trapped in ice for almost one year. The ship sank on November 21, 1915. People found the wreck in 2022.
4. MS *Explorer* was a cruise ship. It hit underwater ice and sank on November 23, 2007.

GLOSSARY

crew: A group of people who work on a ship.

cruise ship: A passenger ship that brings people to different areas for enjoyment.

currents: Water that moves in specific directions.

damage: Harm.

explorer: A person who travels to discover what a place is like.

icebergs: Large pieces of ice that have broken off glaciers.

icebreakers: Ships designed to clear away ice in frozen waters so other ships can pass through.

lifeboats: Boats on large ships that people use to get off the ships in emergencies.

rescued: Saved from a dangerous situation.

satellites: Objects placed in space to collect information or for communication.

shipwreck: The remains of a sunken ship.

sonar: A device or method to find out how deep water is or where underwater objects are.

whaling ship: A ship used to catch whales and process their fat.

INDEX

TO LEARN MORE

Finding more information is as easy as 1, 2, 3.

1. Go to www.factsurfer.com
2. Enter "SouthernOceanshipwrecks" into the search box.
3. Choose your book to see a list of websites.

FACT SURFER